Between Desert Seasons

Between Desert Seasons

POEMS

Ellen Waterston

La Grande • 2008

First Edition
December 2008

Front Cover art, "Waiting II" by Ingrid Lustig
Back Cover Art, "Gecko" by Ingrid Lustig
Cover Design by Kristin Summers, redbat design
Author Photo by Carol Sternkopf
Text Design by David Memmott

Published by
Wordcraft of Oregon, LLC
PO Box 3235
La Grande, OR 97850

www.wordcraftoforegon.com
editor@wordcraftoforegon.com

Member of Council of Literary Magazines & Presses (CLMP) and
Independent Book Publishers Association (IBPA)

Text is set in Adobe Garamond Premier Pro

Printed in the United States of America

Dedication

for all my relatives

ACKNOWLEDGMENTS

The following poems have previously appeared in the listed anthologies and publications:

All Systems Go	*Mothers and Sons*
Cropped Short	*Finishing Line Press Anthology of Contemporary Poets*
Drought Dirge	*Deer Drink The Moon*
Every Dust Mote	*Deer Drink The Moon*
Gateway to Heaven	*Ronde Dance*
Grass Whistle	*High Desert Journal*
Harney Lake	*Deer Drink The Moon*
High Centered	*Deer Drink The Moon, Ronde Dance*
Hollow Hearts	*Hunger Enough*
My Dad Is a Rancher	*Fishtrap Anthology*
Painted Shut	*High Desert Journal*
Patron Saint	*Verseweavers*
Questions of Fall	*Verseweavers*
Sacking Out the Roan Filly	*The Other Side of the Hill, Cadence of Hooves*
Spin Cycle	*High Desert Journal*
Spring Calver	*West Wind Review, Clearwater Journal*
Take a River	*Honoring Our Rivers*
Tamolitch Pool	*Windfall*
The Farmer, the Gentleman and the Madman	*Clearwater Journal*
Trapping Coyotes	*Range Magazine*

Certain of the poems in this collection appeared in *I Am Madagascar: On Moving West From New England*, Ice River Press, 2004, winner of the 2005 WILLA Award in Poetry.

Black Suitcase was performed in concert with cellist Eugene Friesen in Wichita, Kansas.
I Am Madagascar opened an appearance of Maya Angelou in Bend, Oregon.
Take a River was commissioned by and performed at the Cascade Festival of Music on the occasion of Bend, Oregon's centennial.

I wish to thank Caldera, Fishtrap, Oregon State University's Spring Creek Project, and the Ucross and Wildhorse foundations for giving me opportunities and support during the period many of these poems were written and also poets Eleanor Berry, John Martin, authors and poets Kent Nelson and George Venn and author Scott Sadil for their review of and editorial assistance with this collection. A very special thanks to poet, editor and publisher Dave Memmott, and his wife Sue, for their inspiration, patience and guidance. My sincere gratitude to Pattiann Rodgers, Lawson Inada, Kent Nelson, George Venn, Linda Hussa and Wendy Mnookin for their comments and to poet Robert Wrigley for his encouragement: "If you don't believe in your writing, who will?"

Inveterate doer of this kind of thing.

from *Coyote and the Shadow People*,
a Nez Perce story recorded and translated
by Archie Phinney, 1929 and included in *Reading
the Fire* by Jarold Ramsey

Sometime when the river is ice ask me mistakes I have made.

From *Ask Me*, a poem by William Stafford

Contents

PART I Dancing the Two-step

Dancing the Two-step.. 13
Spin Cycle.. 14
Sylvia's Pear Conserve... 15
Painted Shut.. 16
Sheet Music... 17
Dance Lesson... 18
Homecoming... 19
Fourth of July at the Beach 20
Cirque... 21
Cold Storage 22
Tying Flies... 23
Gateway to Heaven... 24
All Systems Go.. 25
Designed to Fly... 26

PART II Kitchen Fire

Split Sheets... 29
The Farmer, the Gentleman and the Madman.......................... 30
Bird Hits Window.. 32
Maybe 33
Thunder Eggs 34
According to Love 36
Sacking Out the Roan Filly.. 37
Questions of Fall 39
Kate on the Subject of Double-teaming with Jim...................... 40
On Empty.. 41
Sack of Birds... 42
Artificial Flame 43
Profit and Loss.. 44
My Dad Is a Rancher... 45
Spring Calver 46

PART III Luck of the Divide

Grass Whistle.. 49
Hiking to Tamolitch Pool.. 50
Duck Dharma... 51
Luck of the Divide.. 52
Week in Review.. 53
Skip's Dock.. 54
The Priest and the Poet at Fish Camp 55
Hollow Hearts... 56
Dust Bowl.. 57
Line Dried.. 58
Harney Lake... 59
Spun Sugar... 60
Drought Dirge... 61
Perseid 62
Never Say Whoa in a Horse Race.. 63
High-centered.. 65
November Sun-.. 66

Part IV Every Dust Mote

Take a River... 69
Native Hand... 73
Millworker... 74
Off into Day... 75
Trapping Coyotes.. 76
Cropped Short... 79
Hannah Fights... 80
Belatedly 81
Every Dust Mote... 82
Love, Mum... 84

Part V Between Desert Seasons

Island Dream... 89

The Gringos Are Gone.. 90

Black Suitcase... 91

The Artist Feels Small 92

Patron Saint.. 93

Baja... 94

Mothers... 95

While Moths Still Drink the Tears... 96

Curandera.. 97

Toasting Susan 99

Canary Fortunes.. 100

I Am Madagascar 101

Between Desert Seasons.. 103

Author biography.. 105

PART I Dancing the Two-step

Dancing the Two-step

Place your hand beneath my angel wing
and I'll follow, follow,
quick, quick,
slow, slow.
Patterns repeated again and again,
quick, quick,
slow, slow.
Like the artist's delicate strokes that trace
the soft surrender of the breast
plied before on now abandoned canvas.
The same half-light eclipsing the thigh,
same palette of caresses, whispered passions.

Quick, quick.
The past is future
tense. Understanding isn't cure.
What fools we are.
What fools we were.
Slow, slow.
Offer your hand high above my head.
I will meet it with mine,
and twirl for you.
I will twirl,
and again.
Quick, quick,
slow, slow.

Spin Cycle

In dayless basement late
last night, sorting colors that bleed
from pure whites—one scoop Kleen;
temperature: hot; water level: max,
high speed, extra rinse. Right then
the single bare ceiling bulb goes out—
as if invisible wet fingers pinched the wick
of the weary filament, ending tedious months
of unblinking, one-eyed survey: wring, block,
fold, starch, crease, drip, bleach, press, press.

It's so dark I can't make out
my thoughts in front of my face, or
the drying rack where still-damp frictions
hang next to fantasies and neglected, lacy
intimacies cycled low and cold. I feel
my way upstairs to you who, at the very
moment the light blew, lifted your left
buttock while rooting the scores of the day.
How do I know this? Aren't you a little
curious what I think about when, all alone,
I hear the cycle click to spin in total darkness?

Sylvia's Pear Conserve

The stock dog tailed a half-moon in the dirt
as Sylvia balanced on the roof of the truck,
rusty red metal puckering under her stocking feet.
She picked pear after pear, later peeled every one,
turning each thought of him slowly, like a music
box ballerina, between forefinger and thumb,
harvest's tawny skin pirouetting onto the linoleum.
Next—pungent tongues of ginger folded into
the fruit. By dark the sputtering mix thick,
ready to be ladled into jars, lidded,
then lowered into the scalding water.

She invited him for lunch, egg salad and sweet
pickle, served at her green Formica table. They
looked in silence out the window, past brindle
heifers, to the top of the ridge where tries
at conversation faltered and disappeared. She saw
him to the door, but not before handing him
a jar of pear conserve. Sitting in his single-wide
he finished doing what he nightly did—news read,
dog kenneled, horses fed. Swabbing the last bit of syrup
with his finger, he paused to consider what it took to preserve
simple acts of love. Sun up, he placed the Ball jar in his glove
box with a note he wrote to Sylvia stuffed inside.

Painted Shut

Here life is meted out in sections. Farm
machinery parked arrow straight. Coming
or going takes right angles. All those tidy,
yellow-bright rows of weed-free annuals. Even
the unimportant knickknack—meticulous
on your mother's white sill, long painted
shut. She excises crusts from triangular
sandwiches, pays the neighbor girl a penny
for every dead housefly dropped into the bean-
bag ashtray—while you, the good son, plow under
miles of dried cornstalks and all thoughts of ever
doing anything else. As your wife, I sit and crack
snap peas on the porch swing and dream...

of circles. Here, only the curlicuing rivers confound
the grid. Well, once, at the county fair, the round trip
of the Ferris wheel briefly lit up your face, softened
your jaw. More time has passed. I can tell because
it begins to weigh something. I smell it like the rain.
The years fill my gauge with a lightness. Some other
gravity pulls me away. For you words are roadblocks.
But they are how I travel. Get off your plow. Talk to me.

Sheet Music

I am your neglected cello, amber
neck of spruce clefing lonely
before the winter window, maple-
hipped body steamed to the desired
shape to fit between your urgent thighs.
My heart-incised bridge that arcs above
the finger-board obliged your ragged
saws of beginning bow tractioned with rosin.
ADGC, ADGC, ADGC repeated to the tick-
tock of the metronome. Primitive moans
pretending harmony.

I fell for the unplayed sheets
of music precisely laid to look careless.
Believed you a mountaineer rappelling off
crescendos, pizzicato across chasms
of feeling, balancing rakish on four slim
strings. The full range of your props implied
as much. But it was for show, cello and bow
on mute display ever since, pretenses intact
so long as nothing allowed to get out
of order. But I am. So tap, tap on the dusty
music stand, sing and shout, and shout.

Dance Lesson

Clap, clap. "And three,"
he shouts, slurring slightly,
his false teeth shifting
from the impact. Patent
shoes are cracked, black
chintz suit stained with sweat.
"And three!" he repeats, hoping
his students' clumsy steps
will catch up to the idea
of a fox trot. "Like this!"

And he moves alone across
the empty dance floor, his partner
resting invisibly in his embrace.
We watch as he joins two separate
notions, real and imagined, his feet
at once finishing and beginning, slowing
and quickening, until all we think
we need to know is within our reach,
simple as one, two..."Worst thing
you can do," he resumes, "is over-dance
your partner." He smoothes his thinning
hair, and graciously sees Perfection to her chair.

Homecoming

My daughter arrives home from her alma mater,
opens her suitcase, unpacks news and chatter, plumps
her favorite pillow, scouts the house for things
of her sister's she deems her own. While she showers,
I lean against the sink. We exchange conversational doodles,
distinctly girl talk. In the kitchen later on, fingers sticking
making caramel corn, we chat about her favorite music
and classes. Then her boyfriend arrives. She packs up.
 "What's wrong?" she asks as she leaves. From the upstairs
window her younger sister teases: "Chicks before dicks!
And return my stuff before you go."

The needles on the tree are brittle. The head is missing
from the angel. The fireplace mantle is a monument to images
of familial perfection, glued fast to holiday greetings. Some
presents never got wrapped. Others never given, not really.
Another Christmas over and done, with not enough girl talk
in those rare moments between sink and shower when my first
born lets herself come home.

Fourth of July at the Beach

Sitting on the beach, stranded by the receding tide,
she hugs her knees to her chest. He yells "No!"
as he dives into the ocean, as though, hearing him,
the waves will behave. He doesn't notice she lifts
the back of her hand to her forehead, her lip glistens
with salt. Had he ever traveled her body with attention
he would have seen the signs of it being too late,
but his curiosity was too mild. He thought he didn't
have to be present to win.

Standing naked on the motel balcony in darkness
soft as cotton she lights a sparkler, the prickly
shower landing on her breast. This solo firework—
a final act of hope. She seems to know better than
most that the end of things is part of the equation.
She tells him she wants to leave. He kneels
on the stained carpet, before the elements
of mistake and perfection, rolls a ball under the bed
to scare out what lies in hiding.

Cirque

Arms extended overhead, wearing a purple-sequined
leotard, I stand on a ledge high above the crowd. They roll
their eyes, crane their necks back to see what flair—
a jack knife, a pirouette mid-air—as I prepare to
jump to my life. Some yell "Don't!"... the fear
of seizing the day catching in their throats. Others
clap and cheer.

I chalk my hands, grab the bar, hang from my
knees, then let go. Flying spread eagle through
the air, I reach the returning trapeze. True,
I have suffered falls. Errors in attention and timing,
that's all. But ask me and I'd do it again—swallow fire,
be sawed in two, or put my head inside the mouth
of every child and lover.

Cold Storage

She stores kisses
like a squirrel nuts,
to have on hand when lips
are sealed in the frigid aftermath
of a warmer season,
to have at the ready when salt
tossed over the shoulder yields
only backward glances.

She refuses a cup of hot tea
because it holds too much
promise, the possibility of tenderness
limited to a season of unknown
duration or temperature. It's too
much for her. So she goes without
tea and other warm wishes,
tells herself she's content
to hole up with stale kisses.

Tying Flies

My heart rocks between cast and
recoil, between feeling and knowing,
loving and losing. It's the moment
we describe with our lives—the bamboo
rod signaling the nylon line to make
the caddis dance along ancient
channels sculpted by tired salmon
returning home.

I trip on my words carefully
tied to imitate the real heart thing.
Perfectly pretending to be what
you most crave: the yarn like
body, the feather like wings.
But you refuse to bite, find
my lures too dull to hook even
you, the weariest of travelers.

Gateway to Heaven

The woman wearing too much rouge, serving
beer to some locals—spinning, drunk,
on stationary stools—tells me to write
my address on a dollar, put a tack through
George's nose, wrap the bill around a quarter
and throw it at the ceiling. A few tries,
and it sticks, joining hundreds on high
whose folded wings had slowly opened
in deference to gravity and time.

"Guarantees an invite to the be all and end all
party," she said. "This place like heaven to us,
but it's time to move on." Four mugs are raised
in boozy confirmation. "When the buyer appears,
we're celebrating. Everyone who made it up
there gets an invitation." "Shit," slurs one. Afraid
of being left behind he stubs out his cigarette, aims
his hand at his pocket for a buck. Who'd have guessed
the gates to heaven would be so sublimely disguised:
a bar east of Joseph, coming off the rise from Salt Creek.

All Systems Go

Blast off!
A sliver of a ship but fiery, a meteor in reverse,
against all odds, leaves the surface of the earth.
Then, the long quiet—recorded by a thin plume
of smoke. The aftermath an incandescent hope.
At first what I feel is the thrill of watching
a rocket leave home base. Young explorer catapulted
into space to go and do...who knew? It seems forever
before those of us watching feel the repercussion
of what is done in our name. By the time we hear
the fractured roar, those on board have already been pulled
in other directions, answered to other attractions,
even launched rockets of their own whose
flight the mother ship could not control nor condone.

As I see my son out the door, fired by all life holds
in store, my thin wave like a feather in the air—
it will be a long silent time before I fully
sound this leaving. Tender stages of loving,
delayed reaction, afterthought, heard too late
to do anything about. He's off, but I won't believe
my eyes until he supplies the sound of a man-
child striking out on his own. "Good-bye!" he says.
I sign thumbs up. All systems go.

Designed to Fly

After ten hours of trying
the instructor undid
my fingers, peeled
them one by one
off the joystick.
"You don't need
to hold the plane
in the air," he advised.
"It's designed to fly.
A hint of aileron,
a touch of rudder,
is all that is required."

I looked at him
like I'd seen God.
Those props and struts
he mentioned, they too,
I realized, all contrived.
I grew dizzy
from the elevation,
from looking so far
down at the surmise:
the airspeed of faith
underlies everything.
Lives are designed
to fly.

PART II Kitchen Fire

—

Split Sheets

Say my name next time we split sheets
or it starts to feel like some farm boy
fantasy—ass and tit. Say my name.

I'm talking to you, Mr. Zoom, heading off to Greeley,
drumming your fingers on your knee
to the insistent beat of your full throttle ambition
that blows you Willie and Waylon like milkweed.

Meanwhile, I'll be putting cat food
out on the porch in a pie tin,
snapping denim jeans to a crease,
going to work, tending children,
folding sheets, like breathing out and in.

The Farmer, the Gentleman, and the Madman

I The Farmer

"We can't get lost because we've never been here before," is how he put it.
And he reached his hand down into the earth
and dealt the grains through his fingers,
organizing the sod according to suit,
deciding potatoes would be happy here.

"A man can figure a lot of things plowing circles at 1.4 miles per hour," is how he put it.
And he traced the history of the wells along
dirt ditches, inside the delicate creases
of the dry hills, until he came to where
the artesian so generously pours out, inviting growth.

"Just passing through," is how he put it.
"Someone else will come along and call this
dirt their own after we're gone," he said,
testing the well, wishing
it would be different this time.

II The Gentleman

On her way here, and she wept to remember,
she had listened to the ocean in the hollow of his shoulder,
was carried on the high and low tide of his breathing
to a safe land blessed with such gentle winds
that she dared set sail for places
of unpredictable pain, promise and wonder.

III The Madman

He held her down under the water in the irrigation ditch,
the palm of his thick hand pressed hard against her throat.
He wanted to drown her for barking at shadows
that lay long across the hard dirt circle

where the pickup was parked at day's end.
He tried to take her life.
He tried, how he tried.
His wife came at him from behind.
Beat him with the handle of the broom.
"Let go of my dog!"
Overcome by the darkness,
she cried, how she cried.

Bird Hits Window

The unnatural gawk of its open beak, two eraser-sized
holes for eyes. The rendering of the collision: Dürer in precision
and detail. The fanned tail, like pressed petals, as if the whole, small
bird had been dusted first in flour—the chalky line of each plume,
wings stretched full-feathered proffering an airborne embrace.
It hit straight-on flying fast from light to dark, headlong
against an unseen reality, something masking as nothing,
something deadly pretending transparency.

My daughter again tonight in drunken flight
from imagined fears, talcum dabbed under her tired eyes.
I don't clean the window, but leave the outline to ward her off
and any others racing hellbent in midair, arms spread wide
in a gesture of despair.

Maybe

Maybe she doesn't go out. Maybe her high heels don't tap across
the tile floor. Maybe, waiting for him, she gives up on the whole
plan, takes her shoes off and walks in stockings that make no sound.

Or maybe she does, leans alone against the onyx counter eating tapas,
the yellow eye of the quail egg staring up from inside a corona of blood
sausage. Maybe she watches people bead like mercury on the marble piazza.

Maybe her bistro glass of thin wine quivers when the subway runs beneath
her feet. Maybe she wonders where he is, or maybe she knows. He's lost
looking at himself in the mirror. Maybe skin is as deep as he can go.

It could have been impossibly sad except for the old man with a cane
who paused in the street and whistled and for the bird that answered him.

It could have been impossibly sad except for the woman in the airport
who cupped the face of her old mother in her hands and said "*Bella, bella.*"

Heart is as deep as she must go.

Thunder Eggs

Three. I must find three. A trinity. One for each child.
I crawl among the volcanic rubble that litters the desert floor,
dig barehanded in the earth for buried thunder eggs, lava core
bombs—scorched, tumbled, cooked and coated—
then spewed and scattered here, the aftermath of molten fire
these rough, pocked spheres of cinder skin.

On my hands and knees I hunt these geodes buried bone and skin-
deep beneath ancient ash. The ones I find evoke my child-
like notions of mothering before, from inside my hot, liquid maw, I fired
infants once, twice, three times, searing, tearing. Then the floor
gave way. Into the pit of not knowing I fell, the molten bath coating
my untried mold with lava so hot it shattered my core.

I was determined to cool the boiling script, to core
and peel the apples of my eye just so. But the inferno duly singed the skin
of dreams that, it turned out, were more about me than them, thinly coated
aspects of self. Finally I stopped to listen: a song so lightly, within each child,
the splintered crystal chimed flor-
escent lyrics, needle threading fire.

I was late to heed the hot words of my fire-
drakes. "Be less in and of us," they hissed, a cord
around my neck, knocking my stool onto the floor.
I didn't hang. No. All this has softened, not thickened, my love, skin.
I forgive me and therefore my child-
ren. I give way, space, take leave, overcoat

flung across my shoulder, the coat-
tails no longer snagged on ideas of should; the fire
of love at last resolved in the chilled
aftermath of the conflagration, when the core
of the matter, the true skinny
of it all is revealed. I am on the floor,

bowing to this new thing, this four-petaled floret,
my patchwork, fatherless family with a new coat
of arms that blazons passage, limb and skin
and hope through fear and fire.
At the core
is the memory of love and in the tomorrow, the gaze of a grandchild.

My grandchild. I cloak and coat
him with my love, am the careful florist and fire-
tender of his core memories and the full and think of his skin.

According to Love

In me sleeps a sense of life lived
according to love, despite the serpent's
tooth served up by careless children,
despite their father's precious deadness
of heart. I'm no Lear, nor queen, not close,
but the same venom stings my veins.

Don't delay too long for if you do,
when we meet again, we're doomed to dine
on pleasantries. The branch broken
from the tree is useless. Sin is perfected
disconnection. I say this and everyone runs.

When I pray, sometimes I picture suckling
the breast of the Madonna, other times kneeling
before the Lord's feet. He says: "The suffering
you don't transform, you eat." This is where
I need some help. I am told more die
of heartbreak than death.

Sacking Out the Roan Filly

He found a mouse carcass floating in the drinking well.
Made him hellacious sick the same day he got the call:
missing roan trapped in the neighbor's corral.
He put down the phone like he'd never used one before,
as if it was something dreadful,
and pushed through the back door to his pickup.
Headed south.
He steered with his wrists, his hands lifeless,
his metal gaze hard-pressed on the road.
She saw him first and freewheeled
inside the wooden hold of the lodgepole corral,
fancy, dancing, tail high.

"That's what you think," he muttered, hauling out
saddle, hackamore and rope.
"Make no mistake,
this time I'm going to ride the hope out of you,
sink my spur into your strawberry hide
until your eyes roll wild and white.
Snare you with this lariat,
then figure-eight your two hind feet.
Sack and flap and hit and stick,
hobble, tie and trip you down,
just to spook you up one more time.
You ain't never going to buck me off again.

"I'm going to shake and snap that burlap,
make you quiver like a bog in spring.
Throw that blanket up and down
like a bedsheet in the wind.
I'll stand in the middle and snap the whip,
make you come full circle, and again
wearing deeper and deeper
the limits of your freedom.

"I'll heave that leather saddle on your back,
cinch it tight, move up alongside your sweaty neck,

and, holding a handful of your red mane,
quick slip my toe in the stirrup while you stand.
There now. I'll be on your back, slick as can be.
At first you won't move at all.
Then of a sudden, you'll let out a bellow,
put your head down and bunch your legs tight
and let go the Almighty.
Helluva lot of try. I like that in a cow pony,
in a fellow desert rat.
A friend to share my dreams:
that shiny girl who turned me down,
a ranch, a string of horses all my own.
No more buckarooing here, there
for gas, a bunk, and some spare change
gone on boots and beer."

Once she quit he opened the gate,
held the reins in his hand like lace.
Let her find her pace, stood the trot,
his weight balanced over her shoulders
to save her for the long hours.
The sun hung low.
In the meadow, big-bagged cows crooned.
His white shirt filled with the evening.
She fixed her eyes on the distant hills.
The scent of sage was bright under her feet.

Questions of Fall

The logs of their house need oiling
to seal the two inside. He extends
his ladder to the second story, a coat
of shellac applied before her questions
have time to dry. Fat chickadees pry
sunflower seeds from inside brittle pocks
and ponder *dee*, *dee* if it's time to leave.
Koi dumbfounded in the frigid pool
can't tell if they are meant to weather
these questions of extreme cold. Cock
pheasants hurry color along the edge
of harvest, unsure if their vestigial wings
can lift them to the other side. And the mare
in heat breathes short and fast, lining her
black nose hairs with frost, tail held high
like one younger. She can't help but answer
the call that puts geese in a V to penetrate
the sky, lays a woman across an empty
bed lonely, provokes a wild gallop across
the frozen field and then a whinnied
shrill, first for a lover, then for anyone
who will answer the wonder.

Kate on the Subject of Double-teaming with Jim

I'm okay with it,
Shot gunnin' for the likes of you, Mr. Jim.
It's a good enough rig:
14 forward,
Jake brake,
cab-over,
stereo.
And I like them velour bucket seats.

The gig?
You say cross-country refrigerated,
out and back,
split down the middle?
Yeh, I'm okay with it.

Just one thing, Jim.
No messin' around with the roadies at the truck stops.
No visitors in the sleeper.
Do you copy?
No falling down dead with Mogen David either.
I could never peel your blubber body off the floor.

And another thing.
No hikers,
and no speed, no snorts.
We're keepin' all ten Commandments.
I've messed with them Mounties once before.
Amen to that.
I'm Lucy Log Book from now on in.

Shit, Jim.
King's X to the nudie air freshener.
Me along, you'll be forgettin' about her.
Jes kiddin', Jim. Don't get your hopes up.
I may drive truck, but I'm a lady.

And I do drive truck, now,
I get behind the wheel, now,
I roll right through 'em.
We'll be keen, Jim.
And you ain't bad, even with your teeth out.
Come on, fat man, we're the duo.

On Empty

He's clever that way, a funnel fashioned from
a plastic milk jug. He upends the four-stroke, empties
it into the red gas can that chokes on the beheaded
2%. Then he bolts the motor to a saw horse, jams the
shaft into a bucket of water and pulls the start rope,
to run the carburetor clean, insure there's no chance
of internal combustion until next summer.

She stands, legs spread, one foot braced
against the pail. The aerated tide surges,
all the right amounts of air and gas—
but blamed inside a space so small nothing
was going anywhere. She grips the bucket
handle. He leans in, grim, forces the shaft
back into the pail again and again. The motor drones on.

There they are, so serious about their self-created
harbor squall in the middle of the driveway.
She bravely straddles the pitch and roll, he valiant
at the helm, not letting the controls go, not for anything.
"Could have crossed an entire lake by now," he groans.
Her fingers cramp. Her shoes are soaked. "Good to know
how far you can go on empty." As if they didn't already.

Sack of Birds

They say when lost in the woods, stay put. So I haven't moved
in decades. But I have mapped my small encampment at the base
of this tree and every night gazed overhead, taken inventory
of the brilliant, fiery arc of meteors. As to all these evergreens,
I thought trees claimed beauty from root and soil. But beauty
like love is homeless. At the very least I have come to know
this. And that the forest is for the tree. What if

I left and things fell apart, would I hear them fall?
My thin shoulder leans daily into difficult questions of earth
and sky. Today, today I will take heart in hand. There's reason
to do so: they say the membrane between the living
and the dead is thin in October. It's my chance to cross over.

Listen. Is that the bark of a bloodhound? Sound of a search plane?
If I have my bearings right, not far away folks carry on up and down
the river of their allotted time here. They'll be closing up their summer
cabins, locking shutters, hanging bunk mattresses from the rafters
to discourage rodents. They'll discard the sourdough starter, break open
the extra flour sack filled with birds that will flutter into the dusk, puncture
soft holes in the night, let starlight through, like pin lights, like lovers
making love to love. It's cold here.

Artificial Flame

It's too late in the season for a fire. Even
so he had her crack across her knee
the dry branches of the dead lilac he axed,
stack them in the summer-swept hearth.
She litters the pyre with white paper
streamers, confettied evidence she finely
shredded to protect her identity.

As she lays down the fagots she can
picture him, the thief, stealing her card-
board archive where she stored proof
of who she is. On the sly, he slices
open the duct-taped lid with his jack
knife. The box (perhaps you already
guessed) is empty save a few silver-
fish that dart into corrugated corners.

She strikes, the fire falters, she strikes
again (the match head lodging painfully
under her quick) but the brisk breeze
through the vacant room is enough to
put out unseasonable flames. He tosses
her a Dura-log soaked in artifice and insists:
"Dammit. Use this."

Profit and Loss

Saw a blue heron back flap a perfect
landing down river there
on a water-logged willow
shanghaied midstream.
Still there, I'd wager.

I was surprised to hear those words
from you. Most nights, pencil gripped
like you think it's going to get away,
calculating per acre profit or loss
on potatoes, you bludgeon everything
with "Goddamn" or "Son of a bitch".

But there's always morning, the view
of the Cascades unchanged.
Mountains startled by fresh white
trumping cobalt sky. Imagine
anything of such beauty
allowed to remain overnight.

You hold the warm rim
of the coffee mug against your lip,
stare long across the fields riddled
with brown russets. The wheel lines
don't miss a beat in their circular
march toward harvest. I pause outside
the kitchen door. The heron lifts
from the mist-shrouded shore.

My Dad Is a Rancher

No. Not any more.
He pissed it all away.
Injected into his forearm the sweet acres of hardy bunch grass,
shot up the ready fields of mint and alfalfa,
chugged this season's crop of slick calves,
snorted Rusty, Ramrod and ZouZou
whose powerful haunches propelled us, lasso aloft.
Sucked deep into his lungs our hardworking dogs,
like Bean, who'd run beyond reason,
heeling cattle in directions they never dreamed of going.
No, he's on his knees,
spewing the bile, the rotten liturgy of addiction.
His backside turned on the loving harvest we promised.

My Dad was a rancher.

Yes he was. A fine one.
There was a day we'd blow kisses to him
as he headed horseback over Logan's Rim,
his wide-brimmed hat disappearing jauntily over the horizon.
The athletic perfection in his work-a-day ballet
as he hazed cattle in and by,
sorting for sale.
Or swinging out and down off the tractor to position a bale.
Or tenderly sticking a thin strand of straw
into the nostril of a newborn calf
to draw out the life affirming sneeze,
rubbing and scrubbing its wobbly wet flanks
to urge the blood along on its vigorous celebration.
Then gently placing the newness of life
before the lowing mother
whose rough and cleansing tongue took over
where your father the rancher left off.

Spring Calver

The sky reels from clear to madness.
Rain, startled from the clouds,
erases the last tracings of snow,
washing down the earth so we can rework
what was done this time last spring.

I can see a coyote trailing his own
shadow along the ridge, eyeing
the carcass of the heifer we finally
gave up on. Threw too big
a calf. Pulled it dead. Her first,
poor thing, trying to calve all
those days out in the hills
before we found her.

He slit her stomach after,
so the dogs could have at...
Oh! The water's boiled away on the eggs.
Be hard by now. Some have
described him that way:
"Hard as a picnic egg."

In the hen house the other day
actually saw a hen lay. Always
thought they set to do it. But she
stood in that cramped little box,
her downy white breast rubbing up
and down against the splintery harshness
of the wooden sides, her tail feathers curling
with rhythmic effort. Then finally that white,
warm egg. Let me tell you, she did hop
out of there. Fled the hen house.
Squawk! Squawk! I couldn't decide
if she was boasting or cursing the trouble it was.

I'm due again in March.
He says: "You're no heifer anymore."

PART III Luck of the Divide

Grass Whistle

cup your hands
like so
a box shape
then a thin
blade of grass
pulled taut
between your thumbs
now blow
blow

a squawk
awkward
bleat
a honk a quack
not
a whistle

squeeze
your thumbs
tighter

a squeal
puny
shriek
a wail a gag
not
a whistle

gently, gently
forget
the sound
supposed
less *try*
instead
just enough
for breath
and reed to make
melody within
the fluted
clerestory
of two hands

Hiking to Tamolitch Pool

The bell-mare muse led the way,
ringing my words true
as I pushed through beaded ferns
into the backroom of the deep wood.

I found river rocks—small, shiny,
black like caviar, and story stones—
red and brown continents inscribed.

The capsized trees along the trail
revealed roots, choked
on mouthfuls of dirt and stones.

Discarded lichen gloves pointed me on.
The subsiding chords of the river
led me to believe I was getting somewhere.

The pool—blue-eyed in an ancient volcanic socket.
Plaits of yellow fronds swayed on the bottom,
like courtesans beckoning me into the maw,
deep, deep, where I risked losing all breath
to frigid truths, to hot-blooded ecstasy.

Here is the place to plant words strong enough
to withstand the molten fire, to leave
a solidified circumference for others
coming later to peer in.

I stripped bare, crouched
deep in the icy blue waters.

Duck Dharma...

...sub-zero night George's summer dock let
go the shore, made its impertinent way to
the center of the lake. There it stayed, giddy
smug, an aluminum ellipsis...

*You there! Where from and to? Nothing
to nowhere?* it taunted, insisting itself
through the thin phrase of ice that tried
to make flat sense, tried to hold everything
frozen in place.

The wintering teals and gadwalls landed
witless on the shiny silver rail. *Lookee
here!* they quacked and twaddled, preened
then slept, feather-brains incubated under
wing, not distracted by how, no recollection
of when, no speculation about here, there,
next or after.

Townsfolk...a different story over morning
coffee at Gravy Dave's. Dock bothered them
the way a slight toothache might. Not right,
it just floating around out there. Over mugs
of black Folgers they speculated about
their unease, on the metaphysical and para-
normal. That is, until the ice melted and George
towed the dock back home behind his Evinrude,
lashed it good to the cleat drilled into the lodge-
pole in front of his cabin...

Luck of the Divide

Worrying the hem of solitude I walk along the creek
bank dodging trailside miter, sword, thorn
and brood on memory and emotion as it applies
to water. I wonder, does Shot Pouch Creek smell
the ocean in this evening's rain, pick
up its pace, imagining every delicious detail of the long-anticipated
watery reunion with lover? Only
to be plummeted
back to reality, its eddying, ancient
envy of Spout Creek—that nothing, that *brook* that gets to run
and stream with Savage, Alsea and, soon, now, open ocean freedom.
Poor Shot Pouch, condemned to
the well-behaved humdrum
of Tum Tum to Mary's River,
then the slog of the Willamette. Just the luck
of the divide,
the slope, the shed,
the draw
of this wrinkled
land
and twisting rivers. I wonder.

Week in Review

My friend Janette has pancreatic cancer. One hundred and ten children
were swept into the Irish Sea. Carnies were caught selling fruit-flavored
meth. I bought a camp chair on sale. A car bomb killed one hundred
and fifty Iraqis. The heat record was broken here today. The monk said to focus
on the breath. The forest is brown with bud worm. I received a complimentary
guide to being found online. My friend Janette has pancreatic cancer.

My grandson turned three. Wal-Mart collected on its employees' life
insurance policies. The price of machetes dropped in Nigeria. Obesity
was found to be contagious. My son says my daughter hates me.
A bridge collapsed in Minneapolis. I got a backstage pass to the
Willie Nelson concert. He is 76 years old. The monk said the palace
of the Buddha nature is within ourselves. My grandson turned three.

I hiked the Zumwalt Prairie. In the last 20 years, ten million female
infants have been killed in India. A farmer rescued a two-day old
girl, her hand sticking out of the soil of his field. I caught
a trout. The monk said nothing from this nor past lives can be
discarded, but must be transformed into good. In the Congo
rape is used as a weapon. I hiked the Zumwalt Prairie.

I know there's love somewhere in all of this. The morning sky was thick
and orange from a fire in the Snake River canyon. I watched
a caddis fly bounce off the water. Scientists announced a drug that erases
bad memories. I lost cell connection. There's a matrimony vine growing
on the empty lot where the motel used to be. The monk asked if I understood
the difference between pain and suffering. I know there's love somewhere in all of this.

Skip's Dock

My mother always loved Skip's Dock for picnicking outside.
We'd bring a blanket, books to read, and money for a soda,
head toward the massive breakwater that defied high tide.

Driving to Point Judith, we turned when the curve swung wide,
skirting salt marshes where slimy plaits of sea wrack floated.
My mother always loved Skip's Dock for picnicking outside.

Old Skip was a fisherman himself and from his briny catch supplied
us with mussels, oysters and blue Atlantic tuna hooked
near the massive breakwater that defied high tide.

Skip's dock had neatly coiled ropes, cleats and bumpers alongside
to moor jaunty fishing boats that had fished or trawled their quota.
My mother always loved Skip's Dock for picnicking outside.

We spread our blanket, settled in. What could be nicer, she exclaimed
as we cracked and ate fresh clams, soon placing another order,
sunning by the massive breakwater that defied high tide.

The hurricane that summer split the bouldered fortress wide.
No trace of Skip or his dock was left after the storm was over.
My mother always loved Skip's Dock for picnicking outside
Near the massive breakwater that defied high tide.

The Priest and the Poet at Fishing Camp

Father Fessio came to this fishing camp
and deemed it a Christian place. I know because
he traced his catch, the ancient symbol of Ichthys,
and taped it to the pantry door. For the benefit
of any doubting Thomas, he included the length:
thirteen inches and, what's more, the species:
Dolly Varden.

I couldn't claim to have encountered Dolly first-
hand, though I too have cast a line into river waters.
So the obliging Father outlined her fish shape,
mouth closed in resignation, eye a penciled X,
useless gills shut tight, lacking the right mix of
watery air. Then he drew her speckles and spots,
added the date when this holy fish leaped into
his net of prayer.

Dolly Varden. Mottled martyr. Sacrificed to show faith
has a place. On that basis I followed the good Father's
example and recast my filament of hope into the deep to see
what words would fall for my lure of feathery thoughts. What,
of my daily devotion to A through Z, I could land to measure
and weigh in my quest to connect the dots between sins
of the flesh and salvation of prayer—there's always a story there.

I grew impatient. How long could I take sounding the river's
diphthongs and consonants, casting about for a verb hanging
in the eddy, a noun hovering, steady, into the current, over and again
my line coming up empty? I later realized it was not the river
churning noisily by, dumb in its devotion to finding the way, but I
who chattered and shook, the disbelieving poet stranded on the shore,
waiting to be found. That sound? My own incessant patter, my own teeth
grinding against granite gums in the deep and dreamy pools
of my Godforsaken imagination. Dolly Varden, Father Fessio, Amen.

Hollow Hearts

Just as his father did, Virgil farms two hundred acres
and mid-summer baptizes his potatoes with poisons
disguised as super heroes—like Tordon or Eptam,
sons of the chemical giants of Cenex and Monsanto.

Virgil bends down slowly over all the earth
as though he's the giver of life, and returns
holding a spud caked with dirt, brown—a baker.
He slices the flesh with his pocket knife. The fruit
is full and firm. No hollow hearts here he determines
pushing the cap back on his brow like a runner
who just stole home.

He watches the pivots spew water over
soil turned on itself, moisten the velvet
loam plied with perfumed toxins.
He scrawls numbers on his notepad, licks
his lips. He knows full well the bargain
he makes, and with whom. Throwing
his shovel in the back he drives his pickup
home, taking the long way around
his hollow heart.

Dust Bowl

Casting aside the forked willow stick the water witch resorts to seeding
the clouds with pouches of silver tied to helium balloons; tries to turn
back the twisting darkness, to make rain, douse the drouth and fiery
lies the faithful swallowed. Free land! Eden! Bring your plow!
But no silver, no prayer can force the heavens open. Even
hard work and hope cast a shadow. Ignorant deeds
make lightning dry, transmute prairie to dust
and the best of us to heedless horsemen
that stampede the night brandishing
a cape of discarded
shadows.

Line Dried

Boiled in bleach, then rinsed, the dishtowels are hung
on the democratic line. Whatever their true feelings,
they, uncomplaining, share clothespins with stained
socks, halter tops nipped at the nape, pick-pocketed
trousers strung up by the cuffs, or shirts—shoulders
pinched into a shrug against an imagined cold.

Pink bikini panties are clipped next to the gaping
bravado of unbuttoned boxers or T-shirts' homilies
turned inside out (tI oD tsuJ). Bra cups with lace trim
fill slightly in the wind, a tutorial in caress. Orange sheets
and pillow-slips luff in a breeze that trades the sugary
smell of line dried for the nectar of wet.

Some pins, unemployed, dangle on the fraying
nylon cord. Others lie broken in the dirt, steel
spring corkscrewing uselessly alongside the fractured
finger of the wooden pincer.

Harney Lake

When the land said stop talking, I stopped
moving, as though words were needed to keep going,
to soften the blow of lava smashed across this scape,
to deflect the unrelenting gaze of land meeting sky halfway,
to guide my deaf hand across rockbound whispers,
to mourn the lupine's colorful daring, now squelched by heat,
and warn the streams, giddy off the Steens,
that from this alkaline basin there is no escape.

Spun Sugar

Whipped Jell-O salads astride red doilies
next in line to pies sassy with rhubarb
and berries, carefully tined with the maker's
initials. Squares of perfection in chocolate
formation foolishly follow lace cookies
and powdered sugar kisses off the edge
of the platter. On the counter, the coffee pot's
bubbling frenzy promises hot brewed. And beneath
the artificial tree—handmade gifts equal to the number.

Years the women have gathered like this
for the Ladies' Club Christmas dinner,
each driving frozen dirt miles past winter's
yellow stubble, Christmas earrings swinging
wildly, baubled glasses readjusted, looking forward,
as they always do, to talk of children and grand,
the new divan, or a double-wide for the hired man;
gingerly skirting all mention of damaged machinery,
borrowed tools, downed fence, missing cattle,
or hearts, returned broken or lost forever.

Spun sugar. A guarantee of friends for the future.
Miles and miles they've traveled together,
so wise, or so tired that different ways
of doing things seems just plain too far to go—
instead, taking solace in spun sugar again this year.

Drought Dirge

One mile up bone-
dry road, bawling
calves trip along-
side mothers'gaunt half-
notes. Phone lines
droning in the heat
sag to breaking
point from the weight
of sere discords.
The ransacked
hide of a deer lies
scored, pitched, fly-less
in the draw, clef
of sun-cured skin
foretelling a waterless future.
The fretted ribs and fractured
femur intone crevasses, flats,
clefts, sand bars, sharp
mountain peaks, ancient
tremor. The hide of this land
is stretched thin beyond recall.
In the parched creek below
an antler pierces the stagnant
muck recording the receding
watermark. I part the scum
with my stick: a buck,
his head still perfectly intact.
With my baton I poke
the lip, the jowl. Loosed
fur, rotten flesh floats
gently off the face, pink,
bloodless. The jaw,
now buoyant, opens—
a sluggish yawn or wide-
mouthed silent scream. One
blind, pickled eye stares up
at everything.

Perseid

In the summer-hot pitch
of the night-charred
prairie the cowhand stood
solo, lonely

for her, his head lolled back,
mouth open like a diner
creamer, eyes thrown
up to heaven.

He trolled black eternity
to spot the spectacular
gaseous shatter of high
diving meteors from some

other consideration, whose
magnetic sling unwisely shot
them into earth's incompatible breath—
to be incinerated without trace.

He hurried inside and calculated
the years of light left him based
on his current latitude. He hesitated,
but not long, picked up the phone

and dialed by heart.

Never Say Whoa in a Horse Race

I The City Girl

A blue jean jacket was for sale in the window, "cowgirl" written in pink sequins across the back. On the front, a silver studded rhinestone rope. "Now that there's gorgeous. How much they want for it, hon?" "$500.00 it says." "$500.00? Well." He sucked air in through his teeth, leaned back on the heels of his snake-skin boots, pictured that jacket across her shoulders. Her hair blonde instead. Nails blood red. Tight jeans separating sassy buns, making the scene on Karaoke night at the supper club, or at the Heritage quarter horse sale.

The city girl said:
"You can have your Dash For Cash, Go Man Go,
fillies and colts that can run. All this talk about old
so and so, whose horse 'brung a million'. You say come
and hear the auctioneer praise the potent and fleet. Soon
you're rising up with the rest of them. 'Alleluia!' you sing
with your checkbook and pen. 'No guarantees, folks,'
the auctioneer reminds, blowing your signature dry.
'Never say whoa in a horse race!' he winks, giving me the eye.
Country boy, you call this fun? Sorry, I don't wear
rhinestone-studded jackets."

II The Country Boy

He'd forgotten to bring a dress shirt. They headed to the gallery opening. She was the subject of one of the portraits, an image of the cowgirl he wished she was. He stood to the side watching. Afterwards they joined the artist at a private dinner in his house as big as a castle. More forks than he knew what to do with and special stools for the artist's dogs to sit at the table.

The country boy said:
"Where I come from dogs have their place. That's all there is
to it. If they don't do their job they get it between the eyes.
That's all there is to it. They move cattle, herd sheep, ride
in the back of the truck, never set foot in the house. Let me
tell you, there was something wrong as wrong could be, to be
seated with a dog to the right and left of me. Their goddamned

63

water served in glass bowls. I don't care how much money
that son of a bitch got. He, like them useless dogs, ought to
be shot. Everyone went ahead and ate their dinner like nothing.
Talked of music festivals, the better schools and such
with them counterfeits setting right up there lapping
and drooling. Sorry, I don't set at no table with no dogs."

High-centered

I was on my long way to somewhere
when, half way between the Equator
and the North Pole, a phantasm
appeared on the low-heeled horizon
of an empty stretch of desert road.

The sign said: Welcome! Ghost town, curios, gas, ice.

I pulled over to check my progress,
idled in neutral on the road side, dead
centered between cold and hot. I told
myself: just a short break in the drive.

How silently time derails here. How fast
I forget to risk, to feel.

Along this, the only street, tattered screens
whistle and mew in the imagined breeze.
Catawampus door titters on a single hinge,
pretending the same thing: wind. Porch planks
yawp and yearn toward the supposed sun.
"Welcome," says the apparition and changes
the sign to read, Population: one
more.

November Sun-

flower stands like stork, stubborn on one thin yellowed
stalk, serrated head slung slack, hangman's fracture.

Her beaded orb cast downward, spent seeds tumble groundward
from its single round eyeball, intent on one socket of dirt in front
of its craned pencil foot, as if sheer-willing pods

of unfinished flower business beneath insulating leaf, mud, snow
so that patiently, later, not now, when March looses the gelid hold, first stirs
the buried, soggy resolve, when all that's left

of the brittle-maned lioness is rotted, crumpled humus, this hunched
Cyclops will have stared down the earth and won
the right to another round.

PART IV Every Dust Mote

Take A River
Bend, Oregon 1905 - 2005

Listen from right here:
the muted falls, the nighthawk's
call, an isolated quack, the heart's
skip, lap of paddle, the whisper
of wind through the quiet
colored end of evening.

"Here in Bend, tonight,"
said *Bulletin* publisher
George Putnam in 1913,
"we envy no one."
He is still right.

Take a river and bend it,
a dream and transcend it.
Take adventure and seek it,
an idea and build it. January
1905. In light and city years,
Bend, you're so young. Stop
for a moment to run a finger
along the dusty shelf of history,
step in the footprint of cork
boot, leather brogan, beaded
moccasin to see where we
have been, where we might go.

Ta-ma-no-hus chuck, this magical river.
Skoo-kum sagh-a-lie ill-a-hee: mighty mountains.
To-ke-tie: so pretty. *Pol-ak-lie*: this night.

Chief Chinook, Chief Paulina, you fished
along this heron-priested shore, hunted
deer and elk on stealthy feet. Did you
not see the greed of trappers reaping
a Deschutes fat with fish and beaver?
Did you not hear the alarm of ox-cart

wheels? Homesteaders, thousands,
crossed a continent in wagons and carts
for land that is one third rock; for a chance
to stake their claim to hope, pulled
behind horse-drawn plow and rake.

Farewell Bend, Thomas Clark named it—1851.
A place for these prairie schooners to port,
to clear land for dreams, to write ambition
in thin, blue flumes of river water Alexander
Drake channeled across this dry land.

Life then hard on proper women. Canned all
scorching summer over wood stoves. Tended
children, milk cow, garden, bonnet brims blown
backward by thirsty wind. They'd lift their skirts
to dodge dirt or boardwalk splinter; never showed
more than two inches of ankle; never walked
on Greenwood and Bond—especially when buckaroos
or herders tangled through town, chasing down sheep,
driving cattle through the streets. It was said
the dust didn't settle for days. When it did
the ladies of the night paid cash for their new shoes.

Bend, an outpost of hope, from range through world wars.
Before 1911 was the biggest empty in the whole country
with no railroad. Shaniko— as far as you could go. From
there a wagon-road south, nothing but rut-holes and boulders.
Passengers would lay hold to help push Cornett coaches
stuck in a bog. Seven hours to Bend on a good day.

These same downtown streets were platted according to wagon
widths: Bond and Wall three across, Oregon and Minnesota
only two. Folks scrambled for seats on the rickety stage,
heady with the sense of going to...who knew? Oh,
the intoxication of: "Who knew?" Who knew
what lay between sleeping volcano, high prairie
and bright water that traced the shores of this high
desert island adrift in Central Oregon's starry deep?
The same year, 1910, that Bend first turned on a light,

captured the electrical might of the river, Harriman
and Hill drove the golden spike, opened wide Oregon's
trunk. Remember how the hiss and steam of locomotives
scared horses and kids silly? No sooner that iron road
laid down than lumber mills rumbled in its wake.
On your mark, Shevlin Hixon! Get set, Brooks Scanlon!
On go! they felled and skidded red-chested logs out
of forgiving forests. Down the Deschutes they rogued
and jammed. 1915—Bend, a timber town. Stirred
its coffee with its thumb! Ring up on the party line
and tell everyone. The men of Bemidji and Bowstring
heard the call. Loaded their families to hob and nail,
cut and trim a better life for all of them. The din of cars
and buggies crowded the widening reach of streets
and homes. Deals were made on the porch of Pilot
Butte Inn. The glow of Mill A's wigwam lit the pitch
boats of young boys' dreams. And their fathers sang
into every day, certain their loggin' woods life was here to stay.

Bend was booming. Hooray and fireworks! In '33
the town celebrated with Parades of Progress. Queens
of beauty floated by, seated on the backs of papier
swan, reflected in the blackened, nighttime pond.

Oh logger, oh planer, oh sawyer did you not hear
the alarm in the mill's whistle? Heed the cry
of the owl? In '94 the last log was sawed
and trimmed, wooden basilicas all torn red
down, save three smoke stacks that reach
straight up into the eye of the sky.

Boardwalks to sidewalks, sagebrush
to lavish scape. Good-bye Masterson,
hello St. Clair Place. Old mill to new,
feast, fest, on the run. Efficiency, top
of the line, doctors and strong medicine.
Pole, pedal, paddle; person, place and thing.
Start and finish strong, right here in Bend.
A newly branded land rush is on! Now
houses, now condos, now centers of learning,

now land trust, now music, now film and writing.
Celebrate invention, amazement, and derring-do.
Harvest sun, snow and all things virtual. Bend
beckons us to regale on a cornucopia sublime
during this our allotted capsule of time.

But where now is the uncharted territory? Where
is the next land of "who knew"? What cries do we
fail to heed, alarms to hear as molten dreams shift
the sleep of the South Sister? Are we more river
than rock? More transient than not? Bend 2105.
The Indian chief would advise: Find four roads
that run side by side and choose the middle
one. Learn to see, eyes shut, with blinding sight.

We are writing the early pages of that spacious
and distant answer. It's a lot with a view thanks
to you: Fremont, Todd, Reid, Putnam, Ogden,
Eades, Egg and Drake; Sisemore, Overturf,
Sather and don't forget Ruth Stover and her
square piano, her husband Dutch, and his
snappy banjo. They showed us how to take
a dream and transcend it, adventure
and seek it, an idea and build it;
to take a river and bend it,
to take a river and wend it
deep in our hearts.

Native Hand

The color of the earth, this hand,
which speaks of root, basket, berry
and, with patient caress,
divines cradle board from carcass,
winnows sweetness from wild rye,
cajoles tools out of bones.
Bronzed riders in streamlined embrace
race wild ponies across this palm.
And across these knuckles,
stick games parlay
the harvest moon away.
The color of the earth, this hand.

Millworker

Curl my arm around the belt.
Throw my leg over the cog.
Press my head against the flywheel.
Cup my mouth to the pump.

My heart beats the treadle.
The treadle sets my hand.
My hand guides the saw.
The saw cuts the log.
The board goes to blade.

Turn my hand to the lathe.
Fix my forearm to the chipper.
Hook my shoulder to the trimmer.
Latch my back to the planer.

My heart beats the treadle.
The treadle spells my name.
The edger names my lovers.
The saw steals my manhood.
The coffee steams my dreams.

Forward, back, swivel, set.
Lower, higher, hand on lever.
Stripped down log one after the other.
Man and machine one and forever.

Off into Day

I called to hear the news of your death from you.
The phone rang and rang, strung rings
around your sitting room, sunny studio,
around your easel, palette, news clips and photos.
Rung around your oxygen tank and wheelchair,
wisps of white hair snagged on the headrest;
festooned your self-portrait, your still life,
and the dark bottles of herbal answers
arranged on the shelf. The phone rang and rang.
The day's letters fluttered to the floor,
forced through the slot in the door
by the mailman who whistled away.
The day's newspaper slapped on the step,
the paperboy's sack chattering against the spokes
as he bicycled off into day.
I hung up the phone. The ringing
stopped and stopped.

Trapping Coyotes

For years I was the only trapper
running lines from Prineville to Suplee.
Checked all fifty miles every three days.
Got around in my old Willy's Jeep.
Hell of a rig.
Seems like we'd get in a different
fix every day. Never gave it much
thought back then, like that bridge that gave way,
me and Willy only half across.
Hell of a rig.

The wife would stay in the camper.
We'd haul it out middle November—
when their fur's starting to set up good.
Park it at one ranch or another.
Day after day
she'd stay happy putting up preserves
or knitting sweaters for the grandkids.
We'll have been married fifty years June.
My Helen, she is quite the Helen,
day after day.

Ranch folk were happy to see us come
set out traps for the sons of a gun.
Coyotes was hard on new calves and leps.
Packs of seven gang up and take them,
you darn betcha.
And one thing about the sneaky Pete,
it's an even match. Not to boast, but
he's that smart. Fooled me often as not.
A finer thinker I'd like to meet.
You darn betcha.

We'd spend the winter in the desert.
If the weather got too ornery, then
Helen and I'd stretch and cure the hides,
otherwise I was running them lines,

chasing coyotes.
I'd mix the scent the summer before.
Came up with a perfect concoction.
The main ingredient was rattler.
Yep. Snake meat—minced and rank. Just right for
chasing coyotes.

Setting the traps is quite a to-do.
Find their spot marked with scat, dig a hole.
Bury the contraption, then cover it
with twigs—careful not to spring the thing.
No sirree Bob!
Spread the scent around. Hell, I soaked my
clothes in it. Any trace of human
smell, you just as well quit. Last off, sweep
up your tracks with a juniper bough,
yes sirree Bob!

Time or two I'd snag one, foot mangled
in the trap, fur straight up on his back.
I'd wave my hammer up and down slow.
His yellow eyes watched my every move,
like so, like so.
Then whack! I'd smack him right on the nose.
stunning him good, I'd stand on his throat
to cut off his air, and watch his mouth
open and close, his feet moving fast,
like so,

in a dead run as he breathed his last.
Some get lazy and shoot the buzzard.
Not me. I'm paid premium for hides
with no holes. Worth the extra effort,
I do suppose.
When finally he'd give up the ghost
I'd say thanks, my turn to get lucky.
His time will come 'round next, most likely.
A person can never know such things,
I don't suppose.

Day would come to take the hides to town.
Ten stacks, twenty each, tied up in twine.
Fur buyers would come in the spring,
gather there at the Powell Butte Grange.
Gosh darnedest thing.
These men in suits come up from L.A.
to wheel and deal with the likes of me.
I made a good profit on each and every pelt.
Gosh darnedest thing,

just to think of them hides trimmed and sewn
together to be worn by fancy
folks down yonder. Did make me stop and
wonder why all the fuss and bother.
All's the better,
if I get to match wits with the whelp,
see some good country, help the rancher,
put white bread on my Helen's table,
and get someone a fine fur as well.
All's the better.

Cropped Short

Once I had hair to my waist.
And when, finally, I had it cut short
I still, for the longest time,
ran my brush past where
the cropped strands now so abruptly ended,
moving it carefully through
the imaginary locks to avoid tangles.
They may as well have been real.
That's how it feels
to have you gone.

Hannah Fights

Hannah Jaffe Wilson
May 13, 1928—October 17, 2004

The cat-faced cancer clawed
and spat. Hannah dug in, back-
lit a blaze of her own, cleared
with type and pen margins she faithed
nothing could cross, dropped elegant
lines of slurry on the malignant
tantrum that hissed toward her.

The raging Reaper lusted for more.
Hannah mustered a bucket brigade
of words dipped in her flowing
hand, held up her poems as fragile
shield. He sneered, pleasured himself,
incinerating each one, searing black hatch
marks across her pallid palm.

From the doorway of Hannah's shuttered
cabin, I survey the collapsed lines,
smell the charred words and silenced
phrases as snow comes soft to those
left standing to ponder a sentence
without her.

Belatedly

Your death brings me to the point life
was trying to make all along:
nothing but now, nowhere
but here, matters of fact and dust
apprehended by strangers
briefly united in shared confession
of their unbearable evanescence in
the brilliance
of the big bang.
Your newfound
eternal sleep
woke me up
to holding
too fast
to letting go.
Wouldn't you know,
not a minute later,
less than that,
trailing your last
breath, I turned
back to forgetting
the grass is greener
where it's watered,
what I get is
what I ordered.
But I can still recall
your smile.

Every Dust Mote

I'm headed for Alice's. It's been five years.
Couldn't get there till now. No good
reason I can recall. I see she's gone...
for good. Rye has run wild, badger
holes pock the road of molten crush
that drifts easy along lush to
hopscotch of house and out buildings.

The garden gate, mourning absent
push of her palm, eagerly warms to mine.
Lonely wind greens to gold, the
creek spawns spring—
lilac, gooseberry, bumble
and quail. Barrels pop
in the sun, hummingbird
makes a run, bees suckle Russian thistle,
corrugated metal stretches and snaps.
Every dust mote carries light on its back.
Every mote carries light.

Haven't seen you in a minute, she'd say even
if a year. Every moment bright. Her eyes
blue prisms startling fires.

Earl, he'd fly over weekly, look
for chimney smoke, the signal Alice okay or not.
One hard winter, she laid herself out flat
in coveralls, cap. Semi-circled her arms
and legs in the snow. Later Earl airdropped
hay for the cows.

Come spring, the sun melted
her angel print. The grass beneath
sprouted wings. Now I lie inside
the fiery circle of her last breath,
feel the hill heave under me.
Her still life hovers over this

high desert push of land,
prow of rock.

I'd been meaning to come. She'd always
said: "Use just a little hurry
in life, in case you are right,
in case you are wrong." Every
dust mote carries light on its back.
Every dust mote carries
light. Every mote carries light.

Love, Mum

Lunched with Mabel.
Raining in AM.
Porch roof leaks.
Glorious PM.
Painted view of Salt Pond.
Grapes in season.
Love, Mum.

My mother's letters were like this.
The fact they were addressed to me,
in her handwriting,
was key.

Off to Boston.
Friday symphony.
No proper hat.
Largo was lovely.

My existence: that remained a question for me.
Self and shadow in perpetual do-si-do,
due to the imprint of her ambivalence
long before I made my eight-pound debut.
From inside out I'd listened to her
whispered discussions of obtaining
ergot from Phyllis to end this unwanted show
of her incautious celebration of war's end. 1946.
So many women delivering, they lined the hallways on cots.

Big party at Brooksie's.
Nancy and Bob for night.
Walked on beach with Cocoa.
Made grape jelly.

She'd hang the cheesecloth sack from
the kitchen faucet, boiled pulp
and fruit within the woven womb dripping
thick, purple blood she poured into sterilized jars.

84

Car getting fixed at Pitcher's,
so took train to Matt.
Sat next to man from Watch Hill.
To auntie's, then home.

I clung for dear life to the slick walls
of her pelvis as the train jostled from Boston
to Philadelphia. She had arranged
for an abortion there. But over tea
her friends advised against it. "What if
he is a genius?" Arthur asked. "In any case,"
Priscilla added, "if it's a girl, Prince Charles
would make a good match." They raised
to their lips transparent porcelain cups
rimmed with thin green vines.

Got hair done in Wakefield.
Did watercolor of forsythias
in bloom. Dug for clams.
Boots filled with water. Fell over!.
After bath, Dad and I had chowder.

"Be like two fried eggs,
stand on both your legs,
keep your sunny side up!"
She sang as she filled the tub,
applied a cold cream mask
over forehead, cheeks, chin. With a groan,
she sank into the bath's tepid embrace—
her breasts, stomach, and pubic hair an archipelago
above the waterline—then draped the washcloth
over her eyes and face, an indulgence she'd read
in the *Ladies Home Journal*. "Hi, Mum!"
I exclaimed running in to brush my teeth.
"Who are you?" she asked, blindfolded.

A girl? A baby girl!
I'd come. You know
it. But am fighting a bug.
And it's such a trip.

Dad got me Aspergum.
I gargled with salt.
Started a painting.
Fell asleep on porch.

After her stroke, she lay on the cot
in the hospital hall her eyes shut, mouth
agape, her hand, a tidal pool anemone,
waving gently back and forth,
tracing yellow forsythia blossoms.

PART V   Between Desert Seasons

Island Dream

Offspring of the Paso Fino pony run wild on this
island for anyone to catch. The brown boys do
and ride at night with their skintight girls astride
magnolia saddles. They canter their lust under red
Flamboyan arbors and the ghoulish-limbed Turpentine
tree, jump naked into a luminescent bay. Water pearls
on the beauties' skin. Fish flash around them fluttering wings
of brilliant passion. Frogs put their tongues to the roofs
of their mouths and whistle the same note out as in. The dream is
nothing changes here, only repetends: the ferry daily to San Juan,
the bells chiming matins, the lazy loop of egrets, silent, aimless arrows
drifting over white sand beaches. This albino ocean has no
tides, low or high. This is the pinpoint around which
all else spins. The mimosa's dried pods mimic
crystal chimes. But to the touch, its lacy leaves clamp shut.

The Gringos Are Gone

Watching his father put on his wings in the dark, the boy slaps his small brown
arms against his thighs as if himself contemplating flight. "Papi!" he calls
to the barefoot man who leaves to fly weightless with joy through town.
Faster, faster and behind

him on a string he pulls up the startled, sleepy sun trailed by cirrus streamers
of purple, orange. Pancho sees him, jumps in his truck with the mounted megaphone
on top. It's not the vaccine clinic, not the *carnaval* he blazons. No. It's the gringos.
Tourist season has ended.

Hearing the news, the townspeople pause, then pick up their straw
brooms, stoke the *horno* to roast tamales neatly wrapped in husks of corn,
whistle a return to harvesting peppers, melon, *cabrilla* and marlin, riding
their small horses bareback into the Sierra, shaping clay pots by hand.

Black Suitcase

The pig's shriek rolls like wrong
laughter before its neck is slit,
rolls before the wind that carries the scent
of Juan who holds the lust of all men
in his crippled hip. He knows it,
gently blows on the chocolate nape
of his mistress, his *querida*.

Ranchero music bounces
off the hills. A boy strums
in the bumperless truck. A girl crests
the hill at sundown. A yelping
bitch is trailed by panting pack.
Pregnant clouds press against
the back of the Sierras. The view

into Manuela's night, on her stomach
in bed, alone, a single light, reading.
The window laced with bougainvillea
red and *amarillo*. In darkness the ripe
mango drops. Fish dance in the phosphor.
Cellophane bags snared by saguaro
flutter like plastic prayers.
Burning dung and orange rinds
perfume her dreams. Waves
crack open the skull of the Baja,
expose shiny, black eyes like caviar.

When Juan returns he and Manuela
mimic the shape of the shell that holds
the soap. Their bodies slide over each
other in the heat. She smells
la querida in his hair. Rising at dawn,
Manuela neatly folds her power
inside the black suitcase, places
it on her head, her hip curves
like a ladle. She walks as tall
as the majestic royal palm
that flowers at midlife.

The Artist Feels Small

Pin-striped brokers wearing black market gold
watches negotiate timber contracts on Russian
forests over dinner in Prague. Medics in white lab
coats wipe fly eggs from the matted eyes of Somali
children under bed nets. Rail thin models giraffe
the Paris runways after a last drag of a Gitane back-
stage. Latino gangs with pierced tongues howl
at midnight in the empty streets of Albuquerque.
And in New York City exotic queens glue silver
feathers to their skin for the gay pride parade.

And I? I search the trash for words to describe,
pile behind me discarded lines, the refuse, the steaming
heap of redo forcing my plastic lawn chair
to the edge of a road lined with dusty date palms
that leads to San somewhere. A *caballero* on his skinny,
bare-hoofed mount quick-steps by.

I'll do what I can to fledge a writer's life of sorts
but these choices are hard. It started when I was small,
and downstairs heard others' voices or, forgotten inside
my dark and airless playhouse in the middle of the living
room floor, listened in on their conversations. It started when
I stopped to watch the galloping river from a motionless
shore, listened to its instantaneous hello, good-bye.

Patron Saint

She quiets her baby with beer,
the eve of the festival of Saint Pilar.
Urchins jam the shadows like startled fish.
Barks of dump dogs curdle in the hem of darkness.
Old men lean on crooked canes and crow: *Gallo!*
Pelea! Pelea! Ten centavos at the gate, she slips

inside the stark circle of light.
Bird handlers cradle
brightly feathered cocks.
Trainers open ornate, satin-lined
boxes, each choosing a single, silver blade.
Showing off, slice keen slowly across
extended tongue. From pockets, pull red
waxy thread, tie steel to black talon,
knot jerked solid. She holds her baby
to her chest and calls out her bid.

Making rounds, the fat bet collector
grabs her breast. She yields him all
she made selling flour tortillas. He thieves
a kiss and leaves. Fingering her
rosary she rocks her baby, prays
to Saint Pilar for luck, her bird to win.

The trainers haze the roosters to circle's center.
A pistol shot straight-armed at the dark—it's begun.
Feather geyser erupts, cocks spike, jab, cut.
Her bird is down—jittery, panting, bleeding
from the neck. Plucked up, quick,
whole head stuck in trainer's mouth.
He blows air through the tiny beak,
forces blood out of drowning lungs,
to eke a final match from the living dead.

Pelea! Pelea! Cocks explode mid-air,
jump and spur. The crowd is mad
for more blood-stained dirt, until death
does its part. As proof one limp bird
is carried off. She collects her profits.
On her way out, she signs the cross.

Baja

Cactus top
a vulture preens,
neck crooked under black wing.
Loosed, a single feather floats,
turning slowly on itself,
riding the strand of air
that escapes the nostril of the sleeping lizard.

Mothers

I mean no harm. I hope they know,
As I paddle across the ocean bay
Searching for migrating grey whales, babies in tow.

Next to my skiff a barnacled mother breaches powerful, slow,
Regards me with one wild, fist-sized eye as if to say:
"If you don't come in peace I'll have your scow."

Holding the gunwales I meet her gaze and mother to mother declare it so.
Nudging her spouting, slickety baby toward me is her conciliatory reply,
Requiting my search for migrating grey whales, babies in tow.

Looking into that intelligent, almond-shaped eye was as though
I looked into a window on eternity—all the world, all suffering, joy and striving on display.
We each mourned, I with my diminutive and she with her explosive, geyser-like sigh,
       that mothers have always bled for peace. This we both seemed to know

Firsthand. That at times mankind's eye seems shut, no
Thought of living lovingly side by side,
Instead war, assault of women, children, slaughtering migrating grey whales, babies in tow.

But we must carry on no matter, that charge the she-whale did bestow,
As I greeted with a gentle push her smiling, mischievous baby's wish to play.
Then she dove deep, keened to her calf, melancholy
       but resolute, from fathoms below while
I continued my search for migrating grey whales, babies in tow.

While Moths Still Drink the Tears

Howler monkeys swing and scream from eucalyptus
to eucalyptus. Iguanas bask on steaming corrugated
tin. On my walk I find a careless fishing line that leads
me back to a barbed beginning. The plan. I must find it
before the cocobolo is all cut down, before the ghost bat
flies into my humid room, before the dying hummingbird
touches the ground.

"Ha, ha!" laughs Arenal, the lava-hearted monarch.
"A million years of boredom, ten years of volcanic
chaos. From belly to earth the beat drums us. It goes
like this—ta dum ta—percussed on the xylophone
of our ribs with the wing bones of the pelican. Fly
into the light with your dusty notions. Life's nothing
but a mangy carnival, a hurdy-gurdy of lies and
promises that flounce like tawdry comets across
the night. Brown breasts offered like fresh bread under
the lush green canopy, cocaine and beer served for after-
noon tea, and the one they call Rusty, black curls
dyed red, wears a wedding gown, walks the beaches
selling kisses to men. This is the magnificent plan!"

I must leave while the anhingas still nest in the mangroves,
while grief and greed have not yet flooded the arroyos,
while the moths still drink the tears of the sleeping toucan.
Out the bus window I see plastic flowers at a roadside shrine.
I read the painted name on the crucifix as we speed by. It is mine.

Curandera

Antonio, Catholico, cada Domingo
every week, rosary, crucifix
around his neck...but today
he bows to the raisined woman,
a shawl draped over her thin shoulder.
The town's *curandera*. God can't
explain her power. He introduces me
as *gringa*.

She dispatches her useless son
lounged against a truck with no engine,
steps over fawning dogs,
reaches under setting hen,
and points with her head
to a shack engulfed in night-
blooming jasmine.

The impatience of her gait:
an obliging wife or whore, answering
without emotion the other's untimely
call, business to be done.
Gringa here to be shown
if she can see what lies
beyond the naked eye.

The dogs petition anxiously at the latched
door. Inside, light meted through thatch
shrouds pale ceramic virgins. Plastic flowers
bloom eternal at their feet. Expired
votives crawl across the dirt, under
a low-slung heaven of spiraling tinsel,
strings of doilies, lights of *Navidad*.

Una limpia? She barks. *Si*, I say. She shows
me to a plastic chair. I sit before
an altar to earth, fire, air and water—
and too, Our Lady of Guadalupe,

whose chipped terracotta eye meets
my gaze. The *curandera's* old breath touches
my face as she traces me with the incense
of copal, then rubs the egg she stole,
like a gambler warming the dice.

With one hand cracks it into a glass of water.
I watch in silence. The yolk drifts whole.
She clicks and chirps, waiting.
Peers with her flashlight.
Leans in, whistles and hums.

Ay! Suddenly. Loud. *Mira*! *Mira*!
At me. Come see. *Cara de hombre.*
The face of a man. *Mostacho.* Drawn in
The mucus contrails of egg white. *Ay*! *Ay*!
Malo. Hombre malo. Robara tu alma,
She keens like a dog. He will steal your soul.
A creature of *la noche*, the night. The orange yolk

undulated innocently, expectantly below.
I see it, the face, *claro.*
She is troubled, trembling.
Who is he, she wants to know.

Toasting Susan

In the center of the dirt courtyard
the sun draws a line across time right
at that place I start to divine my own
insignificance. Right at that place I stand
in full view of the sea turtle burying her
eggs in the sand, the manta spawning
in the shallows, the whale churning out
her calf in warm waters, and the bleached
cow skull that leans against my drowned
cousin's makeshift shrine. I pour a goblet
in her name, leave it on the fruit-crate altar
and walk to the ocean to contemplate
my relative stature. When I return the glass
is empty. I kneel under the black halo traced
by turkey vultures who have nothing but time.

Canary Fortunes

Every day's a street fair in Tlaquepaque! Mariachis
trumpet on street corners. Laughing children launch weighted
rainbow streamers. Stilettoed girls strut past ears of steaming,
blackened corn, dough fried in grease, rolled in cinnamon. "Shoe
shine, you, señor gent American!" the urchins chant. Hammered
silver, ceramic pots under tarps and tents. "You look? You buy?"

An old man holds a cage the size of his fist, a yellow
canary inside. His wife at his elbow wraps small pieces
of cardboard in foil. "Ten pesos el pajaro tells all!" I pay.
He places a crumb at the door, opens the latch. "Mira, for
seed and shelter what a caged bird will do." From a match-
box the bird picks a card. It reads: "You will leave your cage and
fly free!" "But señor," I say, "this fortune is for a canary."
"Ah, *señora*, only ten pesos mas the biggest secret tell!"

The bird plucks another in its beak, hops onto my hand. "*Señora*,
that a bird is in your hand is very importante." I open the silver-
wrapped note. "The mine is dark and deep." "But *señor*,"
I say, "this too is a fortune for a canary." The bird and the man
and his wife cock their tiny heads and look at me. "Si, *señora*, si."

I Am Madagascar

I am Madagascar. I broke off from Gondwana and drifted out to sea.
It feels like 60 million years ago. On my buffeted isle
remnants of times of wholeness isolated to mutate,
baobob, aepyornis. How could I not sense the impending
catastrophe, hear mountains crunch and crumble,
tectonic plates grind, feel the heat of lava coursing
down earthquake-riven slopes? How could I
sit in oblivion on the very ridge that sloughed
off into the ocean. Did I think leaving
was a destination? Did I see no future
in small shifts?

My nails fill with red dirt as I dig up the past,
my own day of *famadihana*—the *razana*,
the ancestors, exhumed and asked for answers.
They say nothing I can hear even though I wrap their bones
in fresh, white *lamdamemas*, even though I lusciously move
my hips to trumpet and guitar against the checkered lime
chorus of rice paddies.

The dead tell me the answer is "over-behind",
Any aoriana. Time is a circle. We are
always and forever the center. All that was, is
and ever shall be. I don't understand.
I am not of this island.

Tavy, the ritual fires, burn on the horizon.
The lemur lopes screaming from the woods.
Orchids curl and wither. The exotic butterfly
loses its loft and pops and sizzles
like a common slug. The parrot has nowhere to land.
Memories of waltz evenings on Beacon Hill
grow dim. My mother's dinner bell
has lost its chime. Satin bridesmaid dresses
turned into curtains hang in the lorn
ranch house. The land and man that seduced
me is serving time. The carcass of the dead calf

101

lies rigid in the sun, magpies finding nothing
in the desiccated pocks. The corrals are all collapsed.
The wide channel I carved with blind passion
the Indian Ocean now claims as its own.
The mail boat rarely makes the crossing.
High-powered freighters with weighty destinations
pass without noticing my wooden pirogue.
My signals go up in smoke. I am frightened.
This time I hear the eruptions, feel the earth
move under my feet, but don't know
which ridge to shun.

I am writing this to you with a pencil
crudely sharpened with a kitchen paring
knife. If you sing for me, sing loud.
I must change my life.

Between Desert Seasons

On a Sunday, just past San Bartolo,
a bright blue pickup leaves the highway,
turns toward the mountains
that form the spine of the Baja.

In the back, six women wear purest white,
black braids swing across their brown skin.
They sing and laugh, their smiles
adorned with gold fillings.

The old man at the wheel,
stunned by his good fortune,
takes the turn with great care
there at the faded mercado sign.

They vanish slowly from view
at the top of the hill, dip like the sun
below the horizon in a burst of brilliant
green caught between desert seasons.

ABOUT THE AUTHOR

Photo by Carol Sternkopf

As a New Englander who married and moved to the ranching West, Waterston grounds her writing in both of those cultural and geographic landscapes. Her award-winning essays, short stories and poems have been widely published in numerous journals and anthologies. Her memoir, *Then There Was No Mountain,* Rowman and Littlefield publisher, was selected by the *Oregonian* as one of the top ten books in 2003, and nationally was a *Foreword* and WILLA finalist earning her an appearance on Good Morning America with Diane Sawyer. Her collection of poetry *I Am Madagascar* was awarded the WILLA Prize in Poetry in 2005. She is the winner of the 2007 Obsidian Prize in Poetry, the 2008 Oregon Quarterly Essay Award and the author of two children's books, *Barney's Joy* and *Tea At Miss Jean's,* Roberts Rinehart Publisher. Waterston is the recipient of numerous writing residency fellowships and honors, including the 2005 Fishtrap Writer-In-Residence, a 2003 Special Literary Fellowship for Women Writers given by Oregon's Literary Arts, and a 2007 honorary PhD in Humane Letters from Oregon State University/Cascades Campus for her work as an author and in support of the literary arts. She is the founder of the Writing Ranch (www.writingranch.com), which supports writers through seminars and retreats, and is director of The Nature of Words (www.thenatureofwords. org), an annual literary event held in Bend, Oregon the first weekend of November.

Where the Crooked River Rises, a collection of personal and nature essays on the High Desert, is slated for publication in 2009. She is working on a novel. Waterston received her Bachelor's degree from Harvard University and Master's degree from the University of Madagascar.

For information on other titles from Wordcraft of Oregon, LLC
please visit our website art:
www.wordcraftoforegon.com

info@wordcraftoforegon.com

CPSIA information can be obtained at www.ICGtesting.com
Printed in the USA
LVOW040826290912

300733LV00001B/88/P

9 781877 655609